How To Get Pregnant With a Girl

The Gender Selection Manual

Cynthia Lewis

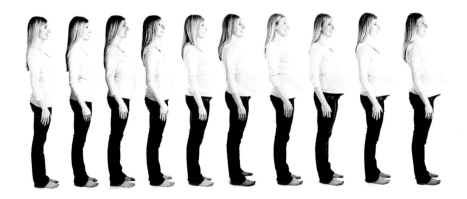

ISBN – 978-1480081925

Printed in the United States Of America

Table of contents

Introduction

You've dreamed of having a baby girl since you were a little girl yourself, playing with dolls. You brush their hair, make little dresses for them and teach them how to talk to boys. Now you're a mother and you have a house full of boys. Wonderful boys, but you still wish you could have that baby girl.

I was in that situation. After three beautiful boys, in fact, after two beautiful boys, I wanted a girl. For the first two scans I didn't want to know the sex of our new baby, but after having had two boys, and now wanting a girl, I did ask the sex for our third baby. When I heard the word "Boy" I felt so disappointed, but as I had had a miscarriage just two months before conceiving this child, I was glad to see a healthy looking baby on the screen. I have to admit that it still took me some time to get used to the idea of another boy on the way. I also have to admit that I felt guilty for having that feeling, but I have since realized that it's a natural response and natural to have a preference in the first place.

Yes, it's okay. Nearly 80% of parents have a gender preference for their child. This preference may change from one child to the next, but most parents still wish they could sway the chances of their child's gender one way or the other. While an equal amount of women surveyed preferred a baby boy as much as a girl, most women wanted their next child to create gender balance in her family. Can you actually choose the gender?

Unfortunately, the sex of your baby is not entirely up to you. Our chromosomes determine our genders: females are XX and males are XY. The mother always passes on one X chromosome to her child and the father determines the other chromosome. Even though the father is "in charge" of the gender of your baby, there are still actions you can take to increase your chances of having a baby girl.

When trying to get pregnant, it can take any healthy couple up to a year to conceive. Know that when using gender selection methods to get pregnant, it may take longer to conceive. Keep in touch with your doctor throughout your conception trials and make sure she knows about any methods you are using.

Once you do conceive, you won't be able to officially determine the gender of your child until you are 18 weeks pregnant. At this time, your doctor can accurately determine the sex of your baby.

There isn't any concrete scientific backing for any of the natural methods of conception, but many families have had luck with these techniques and swear by them. I succeeded and had two girls together. Yes, I had identical twins. The natural methods may not have science to back their claims, but they certainly make the conceiving journey much more fun.

By trying gender selection, many families can have fewer children. Some large families are large simply because the mother and father wanted a baby girl but kept having boys. So, they kept trying without gender selection and made more boys. This wasn't my case. I had always visualized a large family of six children since an early age. Oh, I did warn my hubby about this before he proposed! And no, we didn't stop at three boys and two girls; we carried on to add two more girls. They are all beautiful and I love them all to bits. I can't imagine life without them, boys or girls.

There are some modern technologies that allow parents to choose the gender of their children, but these methods can be very expensive and invasive. Before resorting to high-tech conception methods, try a natural method: a change in diet, adding supplements to a diet, meditating and visualization or alternative medicines and therapies. You can also plan around ovulation times, use a Chinese Birth Chart (That one really is just for fun, I think) or follow the Vedas to help to increase your chances of conceiving a baby girl.

All of these natural techniques can be used privately, in your home. The technological options for gender selection are much more costly and not nearly as private as the natural methods. However, if you try a few of the natural methods without results, a high-tech method might be the right option for your family.

Remember, although some of the methods we are going to discover only seem like fun there have been many positive results from following these methods. You will have to be patient, but determined to stick to the methods. They will drastically improve your chances of conceiving your baby girl.

Looking at sperm – It's about strength, not speed. Dr. Shettles and all that.

One of the most influential fertility experts of the last half-century is Dr. Shettles, of Columbia University's College of Physicians and Surgeons. In fact, he is often considered the father of IVF. Landrum B. Shettles developed the Shettles Method in the 1960s. He published his findings in 1971 in a book called "How to Choose the Sex of Your Baby" which he co-wrote with David Rorvik. Shettles was probably the first person to propose the idea of the "male" and "female" sperm acting differently. He said the "male" (Y) sperm is smaller and faster, but weaker than the "female" (X) sperm. The female sperm are slower but more resilient and can survive for longer once they have been ejaculated into the vagina. They also survive in a more acidic environment, while the male sperm die off.

You can use these differences to your advantage. For conceiving a girl, Shettles recommends the following:

- Shettles suggests having intercourse a couple of days before ovulation to allow the slow-moving female sperm time to reach the ovum while the male sperm die before the egg is released. Then you should abstain two to three days before and on the actual day of ovulation. Yes, you have got to control yourselves lady and gentleman!

- He also said there are specific positions that favor a boy or girl during conception. For the best chances of conceiving a girl, the man should be in a position that puts his sperm as far away from the cervix as possible when he ejaculates. This way, it will take longer for the sperm to reach the egg, allowing the male sperm to die. Positions that will favor conceiving a girl include missionary and woman-on-top. These positions allow shallow penetration that places the sperm farthest away from the cervix.

↻ According to the Shettles Method, women should avoid having an orgasm while trying to conceive a girl. The fluids released during a woman's orgasm can make her body more alkaline, which favors male sperm.

↻ Originally, Shettles recommended certain douches, such as lemon and water, to increase acidity, but he stopped advocating douching due to risk of infection. Douching before intercourse can help make the cervical environment more acidic, favoring female sperm. To create the douche, mix half a lemon's worth of juice with an equal amount of water and use with an empty douche bottle.

This method involves keeping track of your menstrual cycle and knowing when you are ovulating or about to ovulate. We will be looking at ovulation in the next section.

Research done on the Shettles Method shows very good results for conceiving boys. Since the method calls for intercourse earlier than actual ovulation to conceive a girl, the results are a bit lower because any conception is less likely the further the intercourse is from ovulation. 75 to 90% success rate is claimed for this method, but medical experts say that there is no scientific evidence to back up this claim. However, many families still swear by this method and say it works again and again and think of the fun you can have trialing the method's effectiveness!

Ovulation – Get to know your cycle…
The Shettles Method depends upon it.

Planning around ovulation times

All women who are able to bear children have a menstrual cycle. I take it that you knew that! But let's look at this in a little more detail, shall we? The cycle starts on the first day of menstruation and usually lasts 28-30 days, until the start of the next menstruation. During this period there are the proliferative phase, ovulation and the secretory phase. In a normal cycle, menstruation lasts for days 1-4, the proliferative phase lasts days 5-13, ovulation lasts days 13-16 and the secretory phase lasts days 16-28.

Notice I said: "In a 'normal' cycle." This is a general breakdown of the menstrual cycle, but every woman is a little bit different. An ovulation calculator can help you track when you are ovulating to help plan to have intercourse when you are most fertile and when you are most likely to conceive a baby girl.

As female sperm is tougher than male sperm, it can survive longer in the uterus. Having intercourse about three days before ovulation increases your chances of conceiving a baby girl because it gives the male sperm time to die off and the female sperm a chance to reach the egg during ovulation.

Following the Shettles theory, if you do not abstain for the two or three days before and the actual day of ovulation your "girlie" sperm will no doubts lose the sperm race before it starts. Those small and nippy boy sperm will get to the egg first.

If you look at this technically, you are wasting days when you are most fertile, but you are the ones who want to up your odds for conceiving a girl. I did say in the introduction that it may take you longer to conceive if you follow gender selection methods, but hey, it's all in a good cause isn't it?

How do you determine ovulation times?

You need to get to know your body and your menstrual cycle. Reading your body to determine the ovulation day is cost-effective as well as simple and quite efficient.

- A basic ovulation calculator will ask you to keep track of the days you menstruate for a couple of months. If you are fairly regular, your cycles should be the same number of days apart each month. From here, you can calculate your ovulation days based on the numbers above or you can put them in an ovulation calculator online to help determine your most fertile days.

- Another way to tell if you are ovulating is to observe a change in your cervical mucus. A few days before ovulation–the days best for conceiving a baby girl–your cervical mucus will become clearer and you will probably notice more of it. If you are like me, you also have slight cramps or nausea during these days. While the nausea or cramps might make you not want to have intercourse, these are the best days to increase your chances of conceiving a baby girl.

- You can also chart your ovulation with a basal thermometer. Ovulation makes your body's basal temperature rise, so you can determine when you are ovulating. This method only tells you when you are ovulating after you have already started ovulating. If you choose to use this method to track your menstrual cycles, check your basal temperature every month and find when you usually ovulate during the month. Then you will have an idea when to plan to have intercourse to try to conceive a girl.

- If you are still uncertain when you are ovulating, you can purchase an ovulation testing kit at most drugstores. These kits test your urine or saliva for an increase in the luteinizing hormone which is produced by the anterior pituitary gland and triggers ovulation.

Note about prediction tests that they may not be accurate for you and can become expensive.

There are two types of predictor kits:

1. Examines urine.

2. Examines saliva.
   The saliva kits have proven to be more accurate. They are also less expensive because you can use them over and over again. With the urine kits you need to use the first urine of the day whereas you can examine your saliva repeatedly during the day. This enables you to see changes when they happen.

There are some medications that can interfere with your ovulation tests. Check with your doctor to see if any of your medications might alter the results of an ovulation test. Hormonal contraceptives (birth control pills) will almost definitely alter the results of your test. If you are trying to get pregnant, stop using any hormonal contraceptives and wait to try to conceive until your menstrual cycle becomes regular. This may take a few months, but it will help you find out when you are actually ovulating.

Let's go to O+12

It sounds like you are going into orbit doesn't it? Well, perhaps you will, ha ha!

The O+12 Method (Ovulation plus 12) is based on a non-scientific study in New Zealand in 1984 called "A prospective study of the pre-selection of the sex of offspring by timing intercourse relative to ovulation." (By J.T. France, F.M. Graham, L. Gosling, and P.I. Hair). Trying to disprove the Shettles Method, the New Zealand researchers sought to find any real connection between intercourse timing and ovulation.

The couples in the study that wanted to conceive baby girls were told to have intercourse 2-3 days before ovulation. They were told not to have intercourse during the rest of ovulation to ensure the conception date for the purposes of this study. The couples were told to disregard Shettles' recommendations to douche, avoid female orgasm and ejaculate in a particular position.

Each woman tracked her date of ovulation by tracking the *luteinizing* hormone (LH), basal body temperature and cervical mucus. Many of the women found the ovulation dates varied slightly with each method, making the results difficult to interpret. The researchers considered the surge in LH to be the most accurate measurement of ovulation and found that the day before and the day of ovulation were the best days to conceive a baby girl. Notice that this is completely opposite to Shettles' recommendation!

Based on these results, an Australian woman named Kynzi created the O+12 Method. Kynzi had two boys, and then decided to follow the Shettles Method. After four more boys, Kynzi was looking for another way to finally have a baby girl. When she looked at the New Zealand study, she noticed that the day when the most girls were conceived was the day after ovulation had taken place. So, Kynzi decided to try to conceive 12 hours after ovulation and have her husband abstain from ejaculating for at least seven days before they conceived. She finally had her baby girl.

Of the 41 recorded O+12 Method followers, 90% of the women had a successful baby girl conception.

The O+12 Method advises women who wish to conceive a baby girl to conceive 12 hours after ovulation begins. Some people found that these results were better when the man didn't have sex or masturbate for days or weeks before conception. Keep smiling, that man! This is so that you get what you want – a beautiful baby girl.

Let's recap how this method works:

⮑ You must determine your time of ovulation.

⮑ Gentleman – abstain from ejaculation for days or weeks prior to going into orbit, sorry, having that all important sexual inter-course 12 hours after ovulation.

⮑ Only have sex once at that 12 hour time spot.

⮑ No more unprotected sex until you have gone past your fertile period.

Remember, this is not a scientific study and that although there was a 90% success rate reported for the 41 recorded O+12 Method follow-ers, online surveys have not backed up such a high rate. However, there have been successes with this method. It is a question of timing with this one. That might be an issue here. You have more risk of not conceiving at all once ovulation has passed.

If you really do want a girl by natural methods you could give the O+12 Method a go and boost up your odds by adding other methods to it, such as lifestyle change, diet and vitamins. We will take a look at these methods later on.

Time for some fun
with the Chinese Birth Chart?

The Chinese Birth Chart was supposedly found in a royal tomb that dates back to the 13th century. No one is really sure where the chart came from or who created it, but many people say it is incredibly accurate.

The Chinese Birth Chart is literally a chart that shows the age of the mother when she conceived and the month the baby was conceived. When you match the two together, you can find out if the child will be a boy or a girl. For example, if a 26-year-old woman gives birth to a child conceived in September, it will be a girl, according to the Chinese Birth Chart. To test it out, look up your own birth or the birth of your husband or siblings. It is amazingly accurate! It was correct for 5 out of my 7 children when I quickly put in my age at the conception of each of them.

To use the Chinese Birth Chart, look up your age and find the months that conception will lead to a baby girl. Try to conceive during these months to increase your chances of becoming pregnant with a girl.

You can find copies of the chart online or view the original Chinese Birth Chart at the Institute of Science in Beijing, China.

There are some points to note here and there is room for error.

The chart is based on the lunar calendar. The dates shown are according to the phases of the moon.

⮑ For the chart to be more accurate for you, mom-to-be needs to know her Chinese lunar age.

Let's have some more fun with lunar cycles – Enter Dr. Jonas

Dr. Eugen Jonas was a Czech psychiatrist, gynecologist and self-proclaimed cosmobiologist who developed a method for fertility and conceiving a girl or boy based on the lunar cycles. He originally set out to find a Roman Catholic-friendly birth control method using the lunar cycles to help women avoid having abortions. In 1956, he found ways to determine a woman's most fertile times, how to determine the gender of a child based on the conception date and how to avoid conceiving a child with birth defects.

His method says a mother is most fertile when the sun and moon are in the same positions as they were when she was born. So, if a woman was born under a new moon, she will then be most fertile under a new moon. It also says that it is more likely to conceive a girl under a negative zodiac sign. The male and female signs alternate throughout the zodiac, and the moon takes 2.5 days to go from one sign to the next.

The positive male signs come under fire and air:

⮑ Fire – Aries, Leo, Sagittarius

⮑ Air – Gemini, Libra, Aquarius

The negative female signs come under earth and water:

⮑ Earth – Taurus, Virgo, Capricorn

⮑ Water – Cancer, Scorpio, Pisces

Now, I can guess what you are saying to yourself – "It's going to prove difficult to predict when ovulation is going to happen within those 2.5 day intervals." You are right. That is why you would time conception at your lunar fertile peak time. Fortunately, your lunar fertile peak can be calculated and the moon sign can also be worked out for the same time. The Dr. Jonas Method uses astrological charts, known as cosmograms, to calculate these days.

Since most people do not know what kind of moon they were born under, you will need to use this chart with your date, time and location of birth to find out the position of the moon.

Dr. Jonas' method involves finding the specific days unique to each mother that will increase her chances of conceiving a boy or a girl. You will need to buy a Gender Selection Chart online to find your specific days for conceiving a baby girl. You can get a Gender Selection Chart on Dr. Jonas' Web site for about $130.

Dr. Jonas' Method claims a 97.70% success rate. Dr. Jonas discovered that the bio-chemical environment of the endometrium undergoes periodic variations which lead to sperm sedimentation. As a result of this the mother has days in her fertility cycle when she can only conceive a girl or only conceive a boy.

The chart is based on each individual mother-to-be. If you wish to follow this method you will have to send the relevant data and in return you will receive your personal gender selection chart. The chart will show you when your high fertility days are for conceiving a baby girl, not only for this baby but the next baby too (or you may decide to choose a boy the next time – the chart shows you the right time to conceive your next baby, boy or girl).

Once you have your chart, you will see several places where three days are outlined in red and one day is fully red. Some of these will say "Boy" next to them and some will say "Girl." The fully red day with "Girl" next to it is the ideal conception date but you should have intercourse on each outlined day (the three days before the conception date). Once you have a confirmed pregnancy, avoid intercourse on any future days that are outlined in red. According to Dr. Jonas, about 20% of women have multiple ovulations in one cycle and this could result in a double pregnancy, or twins. If you are hoping for twins, then you can ignore that last bit of advice!

You are advised that if the red day falls during your monthly menstruation conception can occur.

Some interesting information about Dr. Jonas:

- Dr. Jonas was sure that certain rules regulated a woman's fertile and infertile times. On 15th August 1956 which is the Day of the Assumption of the Virgin Mary, he discovered those very rules. He checked these rules on various couples and found them to be correct. As he was a devout Catholic he dedicated his discoveries, and those to come, to the Virgin Mary.

- Dr. Jonas was nominated for the Nobel Prize in 1970.

- Dr. Jonas planned all of his eleven children and he not only predicted his last two children's date of birth, but he predicted their births to the hour!

- Clinical tests were carried out and the research confirmed that the Dr. Jonas Method was 98% accurate and Jonas' predicted dates for pregnancies were 85% correct. Not bad. Here are some other statistics of interest. Other doctors used the Dr. Jonas Method with resulting high rates of effectiveness.

- A Hungarian obstetrician, Dr. Rechnitz used the method and claimed a 87% success rate.

- An Austrian clinic using the lunar calculations had a 98% success rate.

- In a Californian study carried out on 800 cases, the success rate was lower, but still at 70%.

Encouraging isn't it? Now let's see what you think about another natural method of gender selection.

Whelan Method

Elizabeth Whelan, who has a doctorate in public health, developed this method of gender selection. Her method says, to conceive a girl, the couple must have intercourse 2-3 days before ovulation, based on the mom-to-be's basal temperature. The mother should eat calcium – and magnesium-rich foods like dairy, ice cream and fruit. Whelan reports a success rate of 57% for girls using this method. This isn't much better than the 50/50 chance you have of conceiving a girl, if you don't follow any natural gender selection methods at all. However, combined with a girly diet and other natural methods, you may wish to give this method a go, to improve your chances.

Whelan partly based her method on Dr. Rodrigo Guerrero, a Colombian physician's studies which were published in the 1970s. In Guerrero's studies, the timing of conception in more than 1300 women was looked at. He used the basal body temperature (BBT) to determine when ovulation had occurred. Shortly after ovulation the BBT rises a little.

Guerrero said that when couples had intercourse on the day when the BBT rose and a baby was conceived, 56.5% of the births were girls. He said that to have more chances of conceiving boys intercourse should take place six days before the BBT rose.

You have probably noticed that this is the opposite to what Shettles says. Guerrero put forward the argument that Shettles used data from studies of artificial insemination and that his own studies (Guerrero's, that is) showed that gender selection based on timing worked differently for artificial insemination and natural intercourse.

If you wish to follow the Whelan Method you need to keep a record of your basal body temperature.

1. For that, you have to buy a special thermometer which measures changes to a 10th of a degree. These thermometers can be found online or at your local drugstore.

2. Take your temperature first thing after waking every morning. Plot the results on a graph to show when the rise in temperature takes place. You want to note when the rise is between half and one degree.

3. You may need to do this during a number of menstrual cycles to determine the actual rise due to ovulation rather than smaller changes in temperature that naturally happen for other reasons.

Best foods for a girl

One thing that has been shown to influence gender is the diet a mom follows. There are several theories on how diet influences your body and your baby's gender. One of the primary ways that diet can be an influencing factor is by changing the pH of your body. Another line of thinking is that different mineral levels can influence which gender you conceive.

Looking at historical trends, it can be seen that more boys are born in times of plenty, when food is abundant. When food is scarce, however, more girls are born. This information can help us design a diet that sways your chances for a girl.

To back this up, in research done by the Exeter and Oxford Universities in the United Kingdom, a link was found between what women eat before conception and the gender of the baby. These studies showed a clear association between a high energy intake and boys being born. The mothers who had boys also had eaten more and a wider range of nutrients such as potassium, calcium and vitamins C, E and B 12 than the women who had girls. It was also shown that women who ate breakfast cereals were prone to having boys.

There are two main schools of thought when it comes to nutrition for conceiving a baby girl. One idea is that the mother needs to eat mostly foods that have an acidic effect on her body and few foods that have an alkaline effect on her body.

The other theory is that the mother should eat foods high in magnesium and calcium and low in potassium and salt to conceive a baby girl. The idea is that this change in balance will change the polarity of the woman's egg and attract more "female" sperm than "male" sperm. Foods that are high in magnesium include black beans, raw broccoli, oysters, tofu, whole wheat bread and cooked spinach. Calcium-rich foods include milk, yogurt, cheese, chickpeas, sesame seeds, salmon and raw apricots. This diet, while it has less scientific backing, is a more balanced diet and may be healthier for the mother while she is trying to conceive.

In addition to the types of food you eat, some studies have also shown that women who conceive baby girls typically skip breakfast and consume less than 2200 calories per day.

Let's look at a diet to increase your chances of having a baby girl, shall we? First, though, I would like to point out that it is important to have an overall nourishing diet that is healthy for you and your baby. Make sure that you take in all the essential nutrients, while at the same time choosing foods which enhance your chances of conceiving a girl. You must bear in mind that a healthy environment is important for your baby. I'm just reminding you to be sensible. Keep to a diet upping your chances for a girl, but do not go overboard and deprive your baby of a healthy mother environment just so that she will be a girl.

Your pH level is important in connection with your diet. A more acid pH will be favoring the conception of the girl, so a "girly" diet is one that increases your acidity.

Here are some recommendations for you:

- Drink milk, milk and more milk – that's three glasses per day, before conception and then continue during the pregnancy. It is thought that grass-fed cows' milk is best. I believe I read somewhere that whole milk helps you conceive too (but don't quote me on that).

- Blood glucose should be kept low. As I said above, I have seen it recommended to not have breakfast, with this in mind, but first thing in the morning it really doesn't make much difference if you eat or not because your blood glucose is high anyway. If you wish to follow the recommendation of no breakfast then that is up to you, but I suggest a protein filled breakfast is a good thing (some eggs for example) for your baby's brain and you will not raise your glucose levels. It goes without saying that you should not eat foods that will raise your blood gloucose – no sugar or carbohydrates or whole grains.

⊃ Acidifying food examples would be whole milk yoghurt, meat, grapefruit, oranges, corn, caffein and pasta (don't eat too much pasta because this will raise your blood glucose), fresh strawberries and raspberries (don't eat the canned varieties in syrup because it will raise your blood gloucose again).

⊃ Some girly diets say to avoid red meat. If you do so, make sure that you eat lots of fish and lamb or chicken. Bear in mind that chicken is less nutritious than fish or lamb. If you avoid meat altogether, make sure that you have enough protein intake with your other foods, for a healthy diet (60 to 80 grams per day).

To re-cap – Each day have lamb or fish. Eat 2 eggs and three large glasses of milk.

⊃ A good example meal menu would be:

Low carbohydrate breakfast – eggs and bacon.
Lunch – chicken salad.
Dinner – lamb stew.
Snack time treats or dessert – strawberries and cream, raspberries in yoghurt.

Why does this work?

A woman's body has a pH balance that creates either an acidic or alkaline environment. The pH scale ranges from 0 (very acidic) to 14 (very alkaline) and our bodies naturally balance in the middle, around 7.36.

In a balanced pH environment, both the "male" sperm (those carrying a Y chromosome) and the "female" sperm (those carrying an X chromosome) have a chance of survival to reach the woman's egg. The "male" sperm are faster than the "female" sperm, but they are also weaker. As a woman's pH becomes more acidic, however, the "female" sperm have a greater chance of reaching the egg and creating a baby girl. The "female" sperm is much stronger than the "male" sperm and has a greater chance of surviving through an acidic environment, while the "male" sperm will die before reaching the egg.

Dieting

For either technique, start your new diet a few weeks before conception. For the best chances of the "female" sperm reaching the egg, conceive a few days before ovulation to allow time for the "male" sperm to die off and for the "female" sperm to have a chance to get to your egg while you are most fertile.

As you eat the recommended foods from either diet, remember that more food is not necessarily better. Try to keep your overall calorie count around or under 2200 calories per day.

Let's have a look at some more food ideas. Following the first diet, you might have citrus fruit and a muffin for breakfast (or no breakfast), corn for lunch and chicken and pasta (don't overdo it with the pasta) for dinner.

If you decide to try out the diet from the second nutrition theory, you might have yogurt and granola for breakfast, broccoli and hummus for lunch and salmon with a yogurt glaze and tofu for dinner. Drink lots of milk and water at any meal.

Watch your pH balance!

Tips for Baby Girl Nutrition

Monitor your pH levels. The first diet is intended to make your pH levels *slightly* acidic, not very acidic. Aim for levels around 6.5 at the lowest. If your body becomes too acidic, it is possible to develop a yeast infection, fungal growth, urinary tract infection or, at an extreme level, infertility.

Once you have conceived, switch back to a diet that will balance your pH levels and give you all the nutrients you need to start your beautiful, healthy baby girl off right!

The second diet encourages female conception but doesn't really alter your body's chemistry. However, once you conceive you won't be able to change the sex of your baby, so you can switch to whatever diet your doctor recommends.

Recommended Supplements

Some supplements can alter your body's pH balance to make a more favorable environment for "female" sperm to survive and thrive. As with any fertility method, be sure to check with your doctor before taking any new supplements.

Nature's Plus Ultra Cranberry Supplement has 1,000mg of cranberry concentrate per tablet. You can take one or two tablets per day the week before ovulation to lower your body's pH and create a more acidic environment. You can also have the to-be father take cranberry supplements to help your chances of conceiving a girl.

You can also take magnesium and calcium citrate in small doses, in conjunction with the second theory in baby girl nutrition and diet discussed earlier. The theory suggests that increased levels of magnesium and calcium along with lowered potassium intake increase the chances of having a baby girl.

Magnesium helps our bodies build bones, protein and fatty acids. We naturally consume magnesium in our diets, but taking a supplement can increase the amount of magnesium in your body and help promote the conception of a girl. This is also a good supplement to continue taking once you conceive, as it has helped some women prevent premature labor. It can help ease stress and insomnia as well. Always check with your doctor first, but you should be able to take about 200mg per day.

Calcium helps us create and keep strong bones and teeth. Most adults need about 1000mg of calcium a day, whether through food or supplements. Keep track of how much calcium you put in your body with your diet, through milk, dairy products, some fish and vegetables. Once you know your daily absorption, take a calcium supplement to increase your intake to 1000mg total. An important part of calcium is how it's absorbed into the body. In order to properly absorb the nutrient, we need Vitamin D. Consider taking a Vitamin D supplement with your calcium supplement or make sure you have enough Vitamin D naturally in your diet.

If you take supplements in the form of tablets, be sure to drink lots of water to help the supplements absorb into your body.

Word of warning if you take supplements

Supplements can help you to make your body a better environment to conceive your baby girl. However, you need to be careful when using supplements. Make sure that you look into them and discover the possible effects of any of the vitamins, minerals and herbs or medicines you take may have on you and, of course, your baby. Be sure to take safe dosage. Herbs are natural but not everything nature creates is safe and that is particularly when you are pregnant or trying to conceive. Alcohol, heroin and tobacco are natural but you would avoid them during pregnancy wouldn't you because of what they could do to your baby?

Discuss any supplements that you are taking or thinking of taking with your doctor or pharmacist. That way you will be safe. Be careful with the dosage of the supplement. Sometimes it will be recommended that you take higher doses than normal; for example, for a girl it is suggested that you take a higher dosage of vitamin C. I suggest that you should begin with a smaller dose and gradually work up to the higher dose. If you discover any side-effects, for example vitamin C could cause loose bowels when you take a higher dosage, then you should begin to take a lower dose.

Another thing to think about is when you take your supplement. Some should only be taken at certain times in your cycle, when you are trying to become pregnant. Make sure that you know if you should stop taking a supplement.

Mixing supplements and any medication you are taking is something to remember to research. If you are taking any medication make sure you ask your doctor about the safety of also taking your vitamins, minerals and herbs. Really, it is a matter of common sense, but it is best to be sure. If you don't feel comfortable with any supplements, then avoid them and, of course, if you start having side-effects stop using them. It is better to have a healthy baby than just go full speed ahead, no matter what, just to get your baby girl.

The list of herbal supplements to avoid at this time is rather long. It's too long to go into here, but you can do research on the Internet, check with your doctor or ask at your local drugstore. They often have leaflets with this type of information. Here is just a small selection for you to avoid during pregnancy:

- Blue Cohosh can stimulate uterine contractions.

- St John's Wart has been seen to act as a uterine stimulant in lab animals.

- Peppermint in higher doses can act as a uterine stimulant.

- Licorice has been known to induce pre-term delivery.

- Dong Quai affects hormonal function and acts as a uterine stimulant.

Alternative medicines and therapies to up your chances

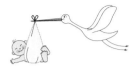

Lydia Pinkham was an American housewife to a wealthy businessman in the 1870s. When her husband went bankrupt in the Panic of 1873, Lydia started selling her herbal tonics to women who had "female complaints." The tonic was hugely popular in the 1880s and made Lydia Pinkham a household name for many women of the time.

Lydia Pinkham's tonic, herbal tablets and herbal compound show some evidence of increasing the chances of conceiving a baby girl. The main ingredients are pleurisy root, life root, fenugreek, unicorn root and black cohosh. This may sound like the ingredients to a spell in a witch's cauldron, but these herbs all have wonderful effects for menstrual and conception issues. Pleurisy root, or butterfly weed, is an anti-inflammatory and carminative (reduces gas). Life root is a diuretic, anti-inflammatory and uterine tonic used by Native Americans for reproduction. Fenugreek helps with wound healing, promotes lactation and is an anti-inflammatory. Native Americans used unicorn root to help improve female reproductive organs and relieve pelvic congestion. Black cohosh is a painkiller, sedative and anti-inflammatory. The tonic also includes about 20% drinking alcohol. Because of these ingredients, women should not consume this tonic once they become pregnant. However, many women have had success conceiving baby girls while using this tonic.

What is the theory behind Lydia Pinkham working for conceiving the girl?

🟢 The Lydia Pinkham compound is acidic in nature and might cause the uterus' environment to become more acidic, favoring "female" sperm over "male" sperm.

- Some of the ingredients, such as black cohosh, may balance estrogen levels. This means to say that if you are estrogen dominant, it will lower your estrogen levels, or it will raise your estrogen level if you are low in estrogen. There is a belief that you are more likely to conceive a baby girl if your estrogen levels are low.

It is advisable to check with your doctor before using this dietary supplement. Many of the ingredients have not been evaluated by the FDA for safety.

If you decide to take Lydia Pinkham here is what to do:

- Followed the dosage instructions on the package or try a half dose. Some people have nausea and dizziness as a side-effect. While taking the Lydia Pinkham don't take any of the ingredients as separate supplements as well. You may overdose on those ingredients!

- Start taking the compound on day one of your cycle (when your period starts).

- Stop taking the compound on the day of ovulation. The reason for this is that black cohosh causes uterine stimulation or contractions. This could prevent the fertilized egg from implanting in the uterus.

- Use of a natural progesterone cream after you have ovulated can reduce estrogen levels and help with the implantation of the egg.

- Lydia Pinkham may cause you to ovulate at a different time to usual, so take care to look out for signs of ovulation so that you know when to stop taking the compound and when to have sexual intercourse.

Lydia Pinkham is celebrated in various versions of a drinking song. Some versions were cleaner than others. Just for a bit of light entertainment and de-stressing I have included some of the cleaner verses here. Enjoy The Ballad of Lydia Pinkham:

> CHORUS: So we'll sing, we'll sing, we'll sing of Lydia Pinkham,
> Saviour of the human race.
> How she makes, she bottles, she sells her Vegetable Compound,
> And the papers publish her face.
>
> Widow Brown, she has no children,
> Though she loved them very dear,
> So she took, she swallowed, she gargled some Vegetable Compound,
> And now she has them twice a year. CHORUS
>
> Willie Smith had peritonitis
> And he couldn't piss at all,
> So he took, he swallowed, he gargled some Vegetable Compound,
> And now he's a human waterfall. CHORUS
>
> Mrs. Jones had rotten kidneys;
> Poor old lady couldn't pee,
> So she took, she swallowed, she gargled some Vegetable Compound,
> And now they pipe her to the sea. CHORUS
>
> Geraldine, she had no breastworks,
> And she couldn't fill her blouse,
> So she took, she swallowed, she gargled some Vegetable Compound,
> And now they milk her with the cows. CHORUS
>
> Arthur White had been castrated,
> And had not a single nut,
> So he took, he swallowed, he gargled some Vegetable Compound,
> And now they hang all 'round his butt. CHORUS

You may wonder why Lydia Pinkham should have become so popular and the subject of a drinking song in the 1920s and 1930s. Well, the compound contained 40% proof alcohol and was available during prohibition. I believe it contains only 20% proof alcohol nowadays, but that is one reason for not continuing to take the compound once you have conceived!

Other herbs commonly used to help conceive are chaste tree berry and Dong Quai to stimulate ovulation and regulate menstrual cycles, black cohosh (in Lydia Pinkham's tonic) and red clover blossom to improve fertility and licorice (the herb, not Twizzlers) to raise estrogen levels.

Reiki for pregnancy

Reiki cannot help you with gender selection but it can help with conception. I received Reiki before conceiving and during pregnancy. Reiki is a universal life force which strengthens a person's energy system. The Reiki healer acts as a channel for the positive healing energy. It is very relaxing and that in itself could aid in conceiving.

It has also been known for Reiki to improve fertility, to the extent of a popping sensation in the lower abdomen during a Reiki attunement, followed by conception and a healthy pregnancy.

Reiki is non-invasive but clears and balances the body's energy flow and is always positive. You receive Reiki for healing physical, emotional, spiritual and mental conditions and then it maintains optimum health. No matter what the outcome, you will feel good after your Reiki session; you will feel relaxed and peaceful. When you are pregnant your baby loves it too, and it can only conclude. I could feel my babies receiving the loving energy.

When you are pregnant, you are not usually ill but there are often certain discomforts that can be alleviated or reduced by Reiki. I highly recommend it.

Reiki is very effective in balancing the shark chakras or energy centers. The basic Reiki positions follow the seven main chakras. If we have a block in a chakra's energy flow, this could lead to an imbalance and to a mental, spiritual or physical disorder. Reiki helps you to harmonize an excess or lack of energy in your chakras. This leads us to the next section.

Manifest your baby girl with meditation and visualization techniques

Our bodies are linked closely with our minds. Have you ever noticed that if you are relaxed and happy you tend to stay healthy? Or have you ever had a loved one who was ill and decided to "give up"? The mind is truly amazing and can have an overpowering effect on the body. Using this, it is possible to "will" your body to conceive a baby girl using meditation and visualization techniques.

For a moment think of your mind as if it were a projector and the screen is reality. When you want to change the film you do not do anything to the screen. You open the projector to change the film. Using the same metaphor, your chakras are your energy projectors. You manifest your reality. Each chakra has an important role to play in manifestation.

When your chakras are balanced, creating your reality becomes almost effortless. The energy is able to flow from your choices and thoughts to the reality that is created. The chakras correspond to particular organs and have certain characteristics. The ability to visualize is via your sixth chakra, known as the Third Eye. The organs corresponding to the third eye are the lower brain, the left eye, your spine, ears, nose and pituitary gland. The third eye governs the seat of the will and thought control along with inner vision.

When the third eye is cleared and balanced, your capacity for imaginative experiences and manifesting them is enhanced. The subconscious mind does not know the difference between imagination and reality. Desire is the beginning of the creative process. In this case you desire a baby girl. As Napoleon Hill said, "Desire is the starting point for achievement, not a hope, not a wish, but a keen pulsating desire which transcends everything." When you desire it badly enough you will commence your path to your goal of holding your baby girl in your arms and welcoming her to your family.

Your second chakra, the sacral chakra is where your creative energies are found. The organs that correspond to this chakra are the urogenital system, the reproductive organs, the legs, gonads and kidneys. If this chakra is blocked or not used very much, you may not have the emotional intensity or energy for you to attract your goals and to manifest them. As I said before, Reiki can help balance this and all your chakras. When this chakra is cleared you can get in touch with your desires and then start the manifesting process and maintain it. The sacral chakra relates to social functioning and a healthy sex life.

The third chakra or solar plexus corresponds to your stomach, gallbladder, solar plexus, liver and pancreas. The solar plexus is connected to dominance, strength, power, fear and thus self-worth. You need to know that you deserve to have your baby girl. This is the key in attracting your desire. To have this feeling of deserving and to allow what you want into your life, in this case, your baby girl, your self-esteem must be at a high level.

If your solar plexus is blocked or weak then you can feel inadequate, fearful and non-deserving. A clear and balanced solar plexus will lead to positive shifts in your energy and your life as a whole. You will have self-esteem and feel confidence and deserving of your desires.

In any kind of meditation or visualization you pursue, find a quiet space where you can sit without being disturbed for 10-20 minutes. Set a timer or alarm for your allotted time so you don't need to worry about how much time has passed while you are in your meditation.

A book called *The Relaxation Response* by Dr. Herbert Benson suggests that calming the mind can help a woman get pregnant. The book advises meditating for 10-20 minutes a day, sitting in a calm environment with your eyes closed. Take slow, even breaths and with each exhale, repeat a one-syllable word. To use this technique in trying to conceive a girl, try saying "girl" or "she" as you exhale.

Meditating with a set intention can take your mind off the stresses of trying to conceive and bring you back to what is most important. In your comfortable seated position, find a mantra, or a phrase or idea you want to establish, to repeat to yourself. This could be something like, "I will have a happy, healthy baby girl," or "I am a wonderful mother," or "I will bring a daughter into the world." Like The Relaxation Response method, take deep inhales and repeat your mantra on your exhales. Repeat as many times as you like.

Try meditating in the morning before you start your day. Clear your mind of any to-do lists, errands, work or stresses. Spend 10 minutes focused inward with slow, even breaths. Meditate again before or after intercourse to calm your mind and your body.

If you feel uncomfortable meditating on your own, there are some recorded guided meditations to help women conceive. The "Guided Meditations for Conception and Pregnancy" by Chitra Sukhu has five songs/meditations to help a mother conceive a baby. While going through a guided meditation, keep the idea of a baby girl in the back of your mind.

Visualization is a form of meditation where you concentrate so fully on an image or scene that you begin to feel the environment you have created through your senses. This can take a lot of practice to fully understand. You probably will not be able to sit down the first time you try to meditate and be able to just concentrate on ocean waves or a baby's laughter. Instead, take small steps. Start in your comfortable seated meditation posture. Calm your breath and your mind. Practice by trying to picture a specific scene, like a rainstorm on the ocean. What do you see, hear and smell? What does the rain feel like? If you feel any other thoughts creep into you scene, don't get frustrated. Acknowledge the thoughts and let them go. Come back to your image visualization.

Once you are able to hold an image for a few minutes, try thinking about your baby girl. Picture yourself holding her when she is first born. Feel her weight, touch her skin and hear her noises. How does she react when you smile?

Stress

There isn't yet any solid scientific proof that stress affects pregnancy. However, following the idea that less stress may lead to a better pregnancy can't hurt anyone and it might just make your conception easier.

Many people claim they conceived after they stopped trying to conceive. It could be the stress of trying that makes it harder to conceive. Again, there is no scientific evidence to back this up, but if you are really trying to have a baby girl it might be the trying that's preventing the conception.

Stress and worry can be alleviated by meditation or Reiki. If you do not wish to receive Reiki you can use a do-it-yourself method. Each of us has a certain amount of healing within our hands. When you feel stressed or worried, you can use the following technique:

- Place your hands on your kidney area. This is where your adrenal glands are seated. These glands produce adrenaline – the stress hormone.

- By sitting or lying calmly with your hands in this position you find that you relax. As you relax, you relieve the pressure on the adrenal glands and slow down the production of adrenaline.

- Try doing this each day for 5 to 15 minutes and you will find that you become more confident and you will increase your self-worth. In turn, you will feel more deserving of your desired baby girl.

Raise your vibration

Reiki transforms negative feelings of lower frequency into positive feelings of a higher frequency. The higher your energy vibration, the better it is for you. Most people suppress their negative feelings and try to not acknowledge them, but in doing so, in repressing these darker emotions, you use up your life energy. When you avoid feeling these emotions you stop yourself from feeling positive emotions too. By regularly using Reiki you can raise your vibrations to a level where you are well in body, mind and spirit. Perhaps you do not want to receive Reiki. That is fine. You have the means of raising your energy vibrations all around you and within you.

You can develop your own ways to raise your vibrations in and around you:

- Start by loving yourself and appreciating yourself.

- Do things you enjoy doing.

- Meditate and breathe deeply; center yourself (feel present in the moment).

- Spend time in silence and take time to smell the roses.

- Laugh – watch something funny or develop a laughter meditation. Laughter is one of your best medicines. When you laugh you stimulate the thymus gland which strengthens your immune system.

- Listen to good music.

- Do regular exercise and keep fit.

- Dance and sing.

- Practice compassion and heal yourself or others with feelings of wellness and well-being.

- Read quality books.

- Have the intent to raise your vibration.

↺ Become healthy in your body and emotionally and mentally balanced.

With raised vibrations you will enjoy your experience, your quest for a baby girl. It should be an enjoyable experience for you both. Feel the love, the joy and contentment.

What do the ancient Hindu Vedas have to say about it?

Long before the ins and outs of reproduction were explored by doctors and scientists in the Western world, the ancient Indian Hindus, in their scriptures, called the Vedas were exploring and setting down guidelines for them in explicit detail. The scripts go back to more than 5000 years ago.

The Vedas have scripts for all parts of life. The Sanskar Vidhi outlines all the major milestones in a person's life. Within the Sanskar Vidhi is the Garbhaadhaan Sanskar, the Sacrament of Conception. To follow these guidelines you don't need to be Hindu, but just believe and trust in the ideas presented in these techniques. Indian families have been following these rituals for thousands of years. The Vedas are based in Hinduism but they are also used as a basis for many Western yoga practices, as guidelines for living a wholesome, balanced lifestyle, no matter what religion you follow.

The Vedas take into consideration astrology and the fact that at every moment every human being is steered by the laws of nature.

In Vedic culture, conception is considered to be a pure, sacred rite that beckons a new soul possessing outstanding qualities and characteristics. A plant on a vegetable patch needs good soil, fertilizer, water and care. In the same way, for the new soul to be healthy and outstanding, the parents, yes that's you, need to carefully prepare long before planting the seed, as it were.

As an aside, according to the Ayurveda the minimum age for the father to be should be 25 and for the woman it should be 18 years. It is suggested that it is best to wait longer than that to allow the man's semen and the woman's ova and uterus to fully develop. So, the longer you leave it, the better "quality" child you will produce. Interesting thought isn't it?

According to Vedic belief, if a couple obey the instructions given in the Scriptures they can willfully obtain a strong, beautiful, intelligent and thoroughly good child. It is necessary to prepare for this and follow certain guidelines including a healthy diet, strict routine, studying of yourself and continence…

1. **Prepare yourselves** – The Sacrament says that heredity and environment have a role to play in the creation of your baby.

2. **Havan or prayers** – Whenever you have sex with a view to conception you need to perform a Yagna or fire ceremony. The Havan should be done before sunset and consists of a series of mantras called Shlokas. Gentleman, these mantras will set the mood for you, as they praise your good lady. They also hale the natural forces, request that the pregnancy be healthy and the child outstanding. This ceremony also involves the burning of cooked food on a fire. Hence its name I suppose.

   I realize that all couples have days when they really do not feel like singing the praises of their other half, but if you want to conceive your baby girl you chant the mantras.

3. **Guidance on which day to have sex** – The sacrament script guides you on which days out of 16 you should or shouldn't have sex and, good news, which days to have sex according to which gender you are hoping for. Very helpful indeed! There are 16 nights for the woman to conceive, from the first day of her period. Here is a list of the 16 days and the results you can expect according to the Vedic scriptures:

The first four days are a no-no! They are impure days. If you have sex during these days, woe betide you…

Day 1 – If you have sex on the first day the man's life span will be reduced considerably.

Day 2 – This is not good for the woman's future.

Day 3 – The fetus will abort.

Day 4 – The father's power will be impaired. A son will be born but he will be poor and miserable and not too bright!

So, as you are sensible you will avoid these days, won't you?

Day 5 – A girl will be born who will probably give birth to girls.

Day 6 – A son will be born, but he will become mediocre.

Day 7 – A girl will be born but she will very likely be barren.

Day   8 – A "noble" son will be born who will be prosperous.

Day   9– A good and prosperous girl will be born.

Day 10 – A wise son will be born.

Day 11– A loose or unrighteous daughter will be born.

Day 12 – A virtuous boy will be born.

Day 13 – A wicked girl will be born.

Day 14 – A rich and religious boy will be born.

Day 15 – A girl will be born who will bear many sons.

Day 16 – An outstanding boy of high intelligence, benevolent and prosperous will be born.

It appears that if you wait until the later days you will have a better child. No other days are considered good for conception and according to the phase of the moon, there are certain days when you should abstain. The sex of the child was thought to depend on the quantity of the man's semen and the woman's menstrual discharge.

According to the Garbhaadhaan Sanskar, men must abstain from sex and masturbation for at least 40 days before trying to conceive. Both the man and woman should follow a pure Sattvic diet for at least one month before conception, avoid drinking alcohol and live a relaxed and happy lifestyle. This includes avoiding work stress, worrying and stress related to the conception.

The Sattvic diet is part of Ayurvedic medicine, a practice that is as old as the Vedas. We will look at this in a moment.

As you can see, the Vedas specify that a couple's best chances of conceiving a baby girl are 5, 7, 9 or 15 days after the mother's first day of menstruation that month. Avoid days 6, 8, 10, 12, 14 and 16 after the first day of menstruation, as these days are considered best for conceiving a baby boy. Obviously, this takes some planning on both the mother's and father's part!

Ayurveda, the knowledge of life

Ayurveda or the science of self-healing is an ancient medicine that developed thousands of years ago alongside Hinduism. It is based on the teachings in the Vedas. Ayurveda literally means "the knowledge of life." Many people still practice Ayurveda today and believe the holistic medicinal techniques create a balanced and healthy person in respect to physical, mental, emotional and spiritual health.

The foods we eat are very important in Ayurveda. There are guidelines for the diet both parents-to-be should follow, but also particular guidelines for the mom and dad independently. According to the Ayurveda there are three categories of food:

- ⊃ Sattvic – nutritious and fresh

- ⊃ Rajasic – stimulating and energy foods

- ⊃ Tamsic – heavy and stale foods

Thus, you can see that it is advisable for the parents-to-be to follow a Sattvic diet for at least one to three months before having sex with the intent of conceiving. Sattvic foods include fruit, grains, vegetables, beans, dairy products, meat and no intoxicants like alcohol.

Since our food is the fuel for our bodies, what we put into our bodies eventually becomes our reproductive tissue, or shukra dhatu, which when combined becomes our children. Some of the shukra dhatu becomes physical reproductive parts like sperm and eggs, while other shukra dhatu becomes ojas. Our ojas are the part of us that helps influence our health, stamina, mental clarity and spiritual well-being. In Ayurveda, the ojas and the reproductive material are equally important in conceiving a child.

As far as the woman's diet goes, she should eat coconut, mustard or sesame oil instead of ghee (a type of butter). It is advisable to have a small amount of barley with your milk and eat more protein and cut down on the carbohydrates.

It is suggested that women desiring to conceive should be slim. If this isn't your case, do not despair. The Sattvic diet will help you on the track to a slimmer and healthier body.

For the man preparing for conception, he is advised that he should be strong and pure. Therefore his diet should consist of plentiful amounts of milk, ghee and rice. He should add nuts to his diet, particularly almonds.

The Sattvic diet means eating foods that are Vrishya in nature. Vrishya foods target the reproductive parts on both men and women, creating healthy sperm and ovum. These foods include asparagus, broccoli, milk, rice pudding, cottage cheese and spices like ajwain powder, cumin, turmeric and black cumin. Both the mother and father should avoid eggplant, tomatoes, bell peppers, coriander, basil and spicy or cold and heavy foods while trying to conceive.

Orgasm or No Orgasm

While a man needs to orgasm to conceive, a woman's orgasm changes the PH in her body. The fluids released during orgasm make a slightly alkaline environment, which favors the "male" sperm. To increase your chances of having a baby girl, the woman should avoid an orgasm during conception.

Before trying to conceive, test your PH levels. You can purchase PH test strips at most drugstores to figure out if you are naturally more alkaline or acidic. If your PH is higher than 7, you are a bit alkaline and if your PH is lower than 7 you are slightly acidic. If you are naturally more alkaline, you should definitely avoid having an orgasm while trying to conceive. Sorry ladies!

Remember, if you aren't close to ovulation and are just having sex for pleasure, have as many orgasms as you can. This can help take the stress out of trying to conceive as well. Remember that you love your husband and can just have fun.

From low-tech to high-tech

I'm Not Getting Pregnant

Take a breath. It can take healthy couples up to one year to conceive a baby even while following fertility and gender selection methods. Keep your doctor informed on the methods you are using. If nothing is working, consider using a high-tech gender selection method instead of a natural at-home method.

High-Tech Methods

There are a couple of high-tech methods for gender selection. These involve doctors artificially choosing sperm that carry an X or Y chromosome, depending on the gender preference of the parents. For parents who want a baby girl, the X chromosome sperm would be combined with the woman's egg to encourage fertilization and a resulting baby girl. Currently, these methods are legal in the United States although they are illegal in some other countries, including the United Kingdom.

Sperm Separation

Sperm separation is just that—separating the "female" sperm from the "male" sperm. Since "female" sperm is a little heartier and heavier than "male" sperm, the "female" sperm can be selected and then artificially fertilize the egg. There is a very high success rate for girls at about 91%, versus 76% success for boys.

The Ericsson Method

Dr. Ronald Ericsson developed his method in the 1970s to artificially select gender in a pregnancy. The father provides a sperm sample, which is then basically put in a race to see which sperm are the fastest. Based on the assumption that the "male" sperm are faster than the "female" sperm, the slower "female" sperm are then separated. For the Ericsson Method, the mother takes Clomid, a fertility drug and is then inseminated with the "female" sperm.

This method costs about $600-$1200 per attempt and has a success rate of about 74% for girls (according to Dr. Ericsson). There are about 25 licensed Ericsson clinics in the United States and about as many abroad.

Density Gradient Centrifugation

This method of conception costs about $600-$900 per attempt and has a success rate of about 65%. In this method, the father's sperm is put into a centrifuge with a liquid solution and spun until the "male" and "female" sperm are separated by weight. The "female" sperm is then inserted into the mother during ovulation.
Several published studies found this method unreliable.

In Vitro Fertilization

In Vitro Fertilization (IVF) is a method used to impregnate mothers with an embryo of a specific gender. This is a very invasive procedure. Mothers must take hormones to stop their natural cycles, and then are injected with artificial hormones through part of the actual pregnancy. The success rate is fairly high for young mothers, but the rate dramatically decreases for women over 30. About 10% of women who undergo IVF have serious complications, including over stimulated ovaries, abdominal bloating and even death.

Pre-Implantation Genetic Diagnosis

Pre-implantation Genetic Diagnosis (PGD), a kind of in vitro fertilization, entails fertilizing the embryo outside the mother, then putting it inside her afterward. This method is very expensive and has a very high success rate, but comes with some ethical dilemmas. Many people follow religions that believe life starts at conception. By using PGD, you are essentially creating several "lives," then discarding the ones that are of the "wrong" gender.

High-Tech Method Conclusions

Each of the high-tech methods is expensive and invasive. Some of them pose health risks to the mother and some have relatively low success rates. Sperm separation and PGD seem to be the most effective methods for conceiving a girl, although PGD comes with potential ethical implications.

Let's get serious for just a few moments and look at the ethics

Sex selection could be seen as interfering with nature–playing god–and as an indulgence.

I do not know your reasons for wanting a girl rather than a boy, but most people who try to select a particular gender do it for serious reasons. These would include avoiding the passing on of a genetic and perhaps life-threatening disease.

The main ethical concern is that with pre implantation techniques, embryos are discarded. This could be considered destruction of prenatal life. This type of gender selection is usually for medical reasons so I do not want to get heavy here. After all we have been looking at natural and non-invasive ways of selecting the gender of the baby and only briefly looked at the high-tech treatments as a last resort.

However, before deciding to try for a particular gender one should think about the ethics and reasons for and against doing so.

Briefly, there are concerns that people will try to influence the gender of their baby for sexist reasons or because a sexist society demands it (this usually applies to males). Although gender selection can mean balance, smaller families and more children having the feeling of being wanted, a boy who knows that his parents had wanted a girl (or the other way round) has to carry that psychological burden throughout life.

There are concerns over the potential for gender discrimination, unnecessary medical burdens and costs to parents and inappropriate use of limited medical resources (pre-implantation and other high-tech processes are usually only carried out for medical reasons, for now). Will only the rich be able to choose the gender of their children is another concern.

However, when you look at nature, she seems to have dealt with all this throughout history. Another concern with gender selection is that emphasis is put on the child's genetic characteristics rather than his or her inherent worth.

I look at it this way– if a couple choose natural methods, for whatever their reasons are, to try to achieve a certain gender baby, then they must be prepared for the worst to happen and be thoroughly prepared to cope with that worst thing. The worst thing is that you will have a baby that isn't of the sex you wished for. If you are prepared to show as much love and welcoming to this baby as you would have to the other gendered baby, ethics do not really come into it. As we have concentrated on natural methods of conceiving a baby girl I do not think we need to get into the heavy discussion over the high-tech pre – implantation method's ethics, as you would probably only be looking at that for medical reasons and that is a whole different ball game isn't it?

We tried and it worked!

Congratulations, you have a baby girl on the way! Start thinking up outfits and hairstyles, and then brace yourself for those awful teenage years. Chances are, she'll be just as bad as you were. Then she will apologize and you can be friends again! Just joking! Those hormones have a lot to answer for don't they? Dad, you will have a beautiful girl to spoil and Mom, you will have a life companion. How lovely for you both.

So, we tried and it didn't work this time. Dealing with your "disappointment"…

So you got another boy. It's okay! Gender selection methods aren't 100 percent foolproof. You knew that. Now is time to focus on the positives: Is your baby healthy? Are his siblings excited to have a baby brother? Are you and your husband happy? Do you want to try again in a few years?

Some women have said that finding out the gender of their baby at 18 weeks gave them time to cope with any disappointment they had if they conceived the opposite gender than what they were hoping for. I know that helped me. This way, I had time to cope and prepare for a little boy instead of waiting until the baby was born and then having a negative reaction. He was beautiful, with the biggest blue eyes I had ever seen. In fact, he was so beautiful, with lovely blond and curly hair, that people were always mistaking him for a girl! You would think that his blue clothing would have given them a clue! No matter what gender your baby turns out to be, it's more important that you have a healthy baby than one of a specific gender.

If you are really disappointed in your baby's gender, talk to a therapist or join a gender disappointment support group (they do exist!). No matter how you are feeling about your baby's gender, it is important not to project those feelings onto your child. He didn't mean to be a boy, it just happened! Share your feelings with your husband and your friends and recognize why you are disappointed in having a baby boy, and then love that bundle of joy to bits. He will bring you many blessings throughout life (and probably heart aches too, but they all do that). Love is the factor here. Your baby was made out of love and deserves all the love you can give.

One woman said she overcame her gender disappointment by watching home videos of her husband as a child. When she saw how sweet and loving he was as a child, she was no longer disappointed in missing out on a baby girl and more excited about having a baby boy.

If you feel overwhelmed with your disappointment, a professional can offer strategies to deal with your negative feelings and give guidance or a plan for recovery.

Your new baby is your world. He is a unique being, a beautiful soul to bring up and love and be proud of. Your first step is to acknowledge that you are sad or even grieving and realize that it is okay to be experiencing these feelings. You need to say it in a way that is best for you.

One suggestion is to write a letter, explaining how you feel, to the daughter that you did not have, telling her how much she would have been loved, but that love will now be given to your son. Once it is written, perform a ritual such as burning it and scattering the ashes to the wind.

It is okay for Dad to feel disappointed too. It can take longer for Dad to get over the disappointment because he does not have the same bond as a mother and her child.

It is rare that parents do not get over their disappointment. Most parents, especially mothers would not change their baby for the entire world, whatever gender they are.

Check list for improving your odds for a baby girl…

☑ Monitor your menstrual cycle for your ovulation days. Aim to have intercourse about three days before you start to ovulate to increase your chances of conceiving a girl.

☑ Follow a diet that encourages "female" sperm and discourages "male" sperm.

☑ De-stress. Get a massage. Meditate. Find a few minutes each day to be in a calm, relaxing environment to focus inward.

☑ Visualize your dream. Picture yourself holding your baby girl. Feel yourself holding her.

☑ Try Shettles Method or the O+12 Method. Try Dr. Jonas Method or the Vedas.

☑ Check with the Chinese Birth Chart.

☑ Stick with the missionary position.

☑ Is Dad wearing boxers?

☑ Mom, forget the orgasm.

☑ Recognize that these methods will increase your chances of conceiving a girl, but prepare yourself for the conception of a boy as well.

☑ Consider the benefits and risks of a high-tech gender selection method. Is it worth it?

Conclusion

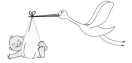

At the beginning of the book we asked if it is possible to select the gender of our children. If we rely on random chance the odds are 50/50. What about if we try to up the odds? Yes, it is possible to sway the odds but you have to realize that it is not guaranteed that you will get what you wish for, whichever of the natural methods you use or combine.

Even without us human beings trying to sway the gender of our babies, it has been shown that Mother Nature follows certain trends when allocating girls and boys. Out of interest and fun let's take a look here:

There is a tendency for girls to be born to:

- Older parents.

- Parents who have more children.

- A mother who is taking the fertility drug, Clomiphene.

- Parents with African-American origin.

- Parents who conceive just after a disaster.

- Anesthetists.

- Fighter pilots.

There is a tendency for boys to be born to:

- Parents who conceived just after a war.

- Parents who are newlyweds under 18 months married.

- Parents having their first child.

- Parents who give birth at particular times of year such as nine months after a national holiday.

- Parents who have more arsenic and selenium in their bodies.

- Parents of Caucasian origin.

- Jews.

As Dr. Jonas said: "The worst that can happen is that a child is born whose sex is the opposite of what was wished for. However, this has happened before!"

Using science and pre-implantation results are just about 100% but this is a costly and invasive procedure which leaves fertilized eggs that have to be destroyed. Most people do not have the money or the inclination for this because they are not comfortable with the thought of disregarding perfectly good embryos just to get the girl they want.

Concentrating on the natural method, who is responsible for the sex of your child? Were you paying attention? Yes, of course you were – it is both parents. We have seen in this book that it is not just a case of sperm getting to the egg. It depends on the environment in the mother. There are different factors involved influencing the gender of your baby, including both parents', but especially the mom's diet before conception, the mom's pH levels and the amount of cervical fluids.

As you have seen, you can influence and change these elements in favor of having your desired baby girl. It is best to combine methods to maximize your chances of success.

All in all, whatever the gender of your child(ren), parenthood is a blessing. With it comes the responsibility of you bringing forth an extraordinary being. You really want a baby girl and if you follow some of the natural methods in this book you will certainly up your odds of having your beautiful baby girl, but be sensible in your quest. Always concentrate on having a healthy, happy baby, full stop.

Remember, both kinds are so very beautiful in their own way. They all have the same needs – tender care and attention, feeding, sleep and the ever important love and feeling of being wanted.

Made in United States
North Haven, CT
21 November 2022

27059282R00030